MATERIALS ALL AROUND US

SOLIDS, LIQUIDS AND GASES

Robert Snedden

Heinemann
LIBRARY

www.heinemann.co.uk/library
Visit our website to find out more information about Heinemann Library books.

To order:
 Phone 44 (0) 1865 888066
Send a fax to 44 (0) 1865 314091
Visit the Heinemann Bookshop at www.heinemann.co.uk/library to browse our catalogue and order online.

First published in Great Britain by Heinemann Library,
Halley Court, Jordan Hill, Oxford OX2 8EJ
a division of Reed Educational and Professional Publishing Ltd.
Heinemann is a registered trademark of Reed Educational & Professional Publishing Ltd.

OXFORD MELBOURNE AUCKLAND
JOHANNESBURG BLANTYRE GABORONE
IBADAN PORTSMOUTH (NH) USA CHICAGO

Designed by Celia Floyd
Originated by Dot Gradations
Printed by Wing King Tong, Hong Kong

ISBN 0 431 12090 0
05 04 03 02 01
10 9 8 7 6 5 4 3 2 1

British Library Cataloguing in Publication Data

Snedden, Robert
Solids, liquids and gases. - (Material all around us)
1.Matter - Properties - Juvenile literature
I.Title
530.4

Acknowledgements
The Publishers would like to thank the following for permission to reproduce photographs: Bruce Coleman Collection: Dr Eckart Pott p11, Stephen J Krasemann p24; FLPA: M J Thomas p21b; John Cleare: p22; Network: Peter Jordan p14; Redferns: Andrew Putler p7; Science Photo Library: p19, NASA p4, Adrienne Hart-Davis p9, Tony Craddock p10, Angela Murphy p16, Simon Terrey p29; Telegraph Colour Library: Chris Simpson p13; Tony Stone Images: Greg Pease p15, Randy Wells p18, David Madison p21a, J Sneesby/B Wilkins p23

Cover photograph reproduced with permission of Tony Stone Images

Every effort has been made to contact copyright holders of any material reproduced in this book. Any omissions will be rectified in subsequent printings if notice is given to the Publisher.

Any words appearing in the text in bold, **like this**, are explained in the glossary.

Contents

What is matter?

Everything that you can see, touch, feel, smell or taste is made of matter. The sun, a running stream and the hair on your head are all forms of matter. Matter is anything that takes up space – whether it be a spinning galaxy of stars or the tiny speck of an **atom**.

A space-walking astronaut may not feel the effects of gravity but he still has the same mass as he does on Earth.

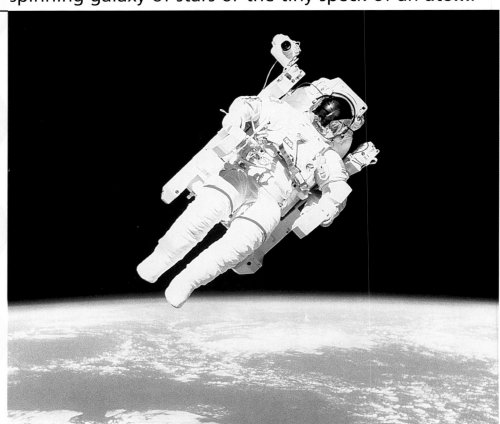

Mass and gravity

The **mass** of an object is the amount of matter it contains. The weight of an object is caused by the force of **gravity** acting on the object's mass. The mass of an object always stays the same but its weight can increase or decrease depending on how strong the force of gravity is. You weigh what you do because of the Earth's gravity acting on your body mass. On the Moon you would weigh only a sixth what you do on Earth because the Moon's gravity is weaker.

There wouldn't be any less of you though. The amount of matter in your body would not change.

Particles of matter

All materials are made of atoms, which in turn are made of even smaller **particles**, called protons, neutrons and **electrons**.

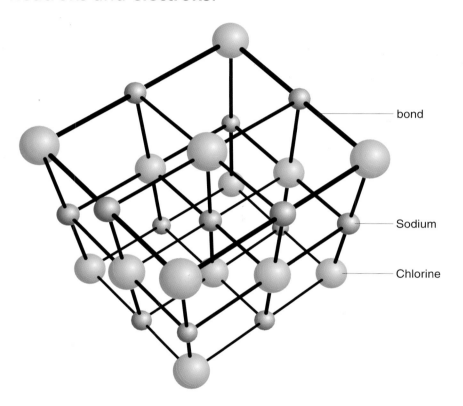

bond

Sodium

Chlorine

Atoms of different elements can link together in a variety of ways to form compounds.

Atoms can join together to form larger particles called **molecules**. Molecules that contain atoms of one kind only are known as **elements**; those that contain atoms of different kinds are called **compounds**.

Molecules are the smallest particles of an element or compound that can exist on their own without being joined to other atoms or groups of atoms. Hydrogen atoms, for example, are not found on their own. They are joined together in pairs to form hydrogen molecules.

5

Changing states

Matter is usually found as either a solid, liquid or gas. Water is a good example of a substance that can be found in all three states in everyday circumstances – as solid ice in the freezer, as liquid water from the tap and as steam rising from a boiling kettle.

The change from one state to another takes place at definite temperatures called the melting point (solid to liquid) and boiling point (liquid to gas). Changes in the opposite direction are brought about by cooling. A gas **condenses** into a liquid, a liquid freezes into a solid.

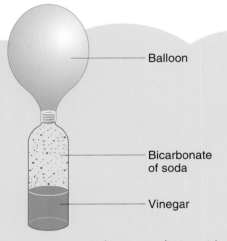

Balloon

Bicarbonate of soda

Vinegar

Try it yourself
You will need
vinegar
a saucepan
a spoon
a balloon
bicarbonate of soda
a small plastic bottle

1 Warm the vinegar in a saucepan and pour into the bottle until it is about a quarter full.
2 Put 1 spoonful of bicarbonate of soda into the balloon.
3 While holding the balloon carefully, so that the bicarbonate of soda does not fall out, stretch the neck of the balloon over the neck of the bottle.
4 Quickly lift the balloon so that the bicarbonate of soda spills into the vinegar.

The vinegar and the bicarbonate of soda will react together to produce carbon dioxide gas. As this happens the balloon starts to inflate, which shows that a gas takes up a greater volume than the same amount of a solid or a liquid.

Latent heat

A substance can be changed from one state to another by raising or lowering its temperature. When a solid changes to a liquid heat is taken in. When the liquid changes back to a solid the same amount of heat is given out. This is called the **latent heat** of the substance.

Sublimation

Sublimation is an unusual change of state in which a solid changes directly to a gas without first becoming a liquid. For example, solid carbon dioxide (sometimes called dry ice) sublimes to carbon dioxide gas. When the gas is cooled it becomes a solid again.

Solid carbon dioxide, dry ice, is often used to create smoke effects on stage as it turns into a gas.

Solids

Solids have a definite shape and **volume**. Solid objects such as stone are rigid and hard and will keep their shape unless a physical force acts to change them. Some solids are **brittle** and will shatter when struck. Metals are malleable (they have the ability to be beaten into thin sheets) and ductile (they can be drawn into wires).

The properties of a solid depend on the **particles** that make up the substance and the forces acting among them. The **atoms** in almost all solids are arranged in regular patterns, called **crystals**.

A slow-moving liquid

Over long periods glass can flow like a liquid. The particles that make up glass can move around, although very, very slowly. The effect can be seen in very old windows where the glass is actually thicker at the bottom than the top.

The atoms in a solid are not free to move but held in place by the forces that bind them together.

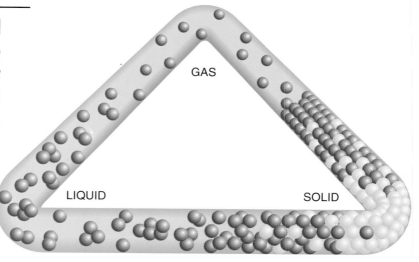

GAS

LIQUID

SOLID

Bonding together

The tightly packed particles that make up a solid are held together by chemical **bonds**. These are the forces of attraction that hold together atoms of one or more types of **element** to form **molecules**.

Melting

The molecules that make up a solid are arranged so that the forces that attract and repel the molecules are evenly balanced. The molecules do not have enough energy to move to different parts of the solid but vibrate in place. If the temperature of a solid is raised, the molecules begin to vibrate more strongly. Eventually the vibrations become great enough to overcome the forces that hold the molecules in place. When this happens the solid melts and eventually becomes a liquid.

The particles that make up a solid are held together in regular patterns.

Liquids

A liquid is similar to a solid because it too has a definite **volume**. However, a liquid can flow to fit the shape of any container into which it is put.

Boiling and freezing

If liquids are heated beyond a certain point, they change into gas. This is called boiling. Water changes into steam when it boils, for example. If liquids are cooled below a certain point, they change into solids. Water freezes into ice. Different liquids have different freezing and boiling points.

Liquids take on the shape of any container into which they are poured.

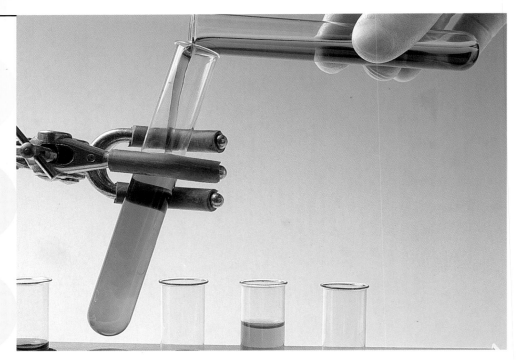

Surface tension

A thin layer forms on the surface of a liquid because of the attraction between the molecules in the liquid.

This is called surface tension. Surface tension is what allows a water beetle to walk across the surface of a pond without sinking in.

Capillary action

Liquids can move into or out of thin tubes. This movement is called capillary action. Capillary action draws water up the roots of plants. Paper towels have millions of capillaries between their fibres that absorb water by capillary action.

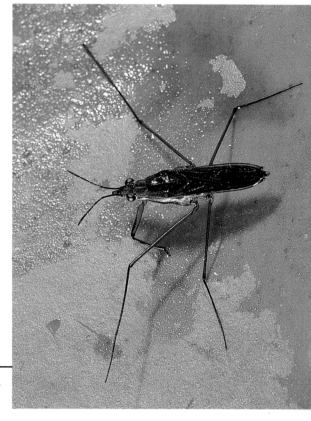

A water beetle walking across the surface of a pond.

Try it yourself

You will need
water
4 matches or wooden toothpicks
washing-up liquid
a shallow dish
a dropper

1 Put some water in a shallow dish and wait until the surface is smooth.
2 Carefully float the matches or toothpicks on the surface together so that they are all pointing inwards.
3 Using a dropper, gently put a drop of washing-up liquid in the middle of the dish between the sticks.

The surface tension in the centre is broken by the washing-up liquid and the matches immediately move out towards the rim of the dish, drawn by the surface tension on the water there.

Gases

The **molecules** that make up a gas are not attached to each other in any way. They are free to move around in all directions. A gas does not have a fixed shape or a fixed **volume**. A gas will spread out to fill any size or shape of container into which it is put.

The molecules that make up a gas are not bound together but move around randomly in all directions.

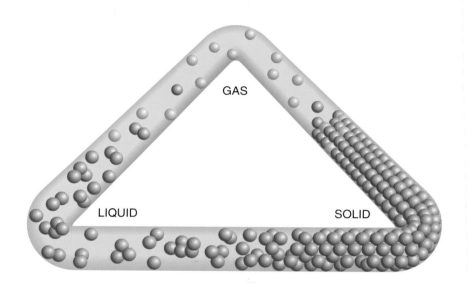

Gases have weight just like solids and liquids. Because the **particles** that make up the gas are spread out thinly a volume of gas will contain fewer particles and so weigh less than the same volume of a solid or liquid where the particles are more tightly packed together.

In the air

Every cubic centimetre of air contains billions of molecules all moving around rapidly. Lighter particles move faster than heavier ones and the hotter the gas is the faster the particles move. The gas particles are constantly colliding with each other and with the walls of any container they happen to be in. These collisions produce the effect of **pressure**.

Gases and liquids

A gas changes to a liquid when it is cool enough for the gas particles to gather together. The temperature at which a gas becomes a liquid is called its condensation point. If the pressure is increased, the gas will become a liquid at a higher temperature.

Gas laws

Gases behave according to three rules, or laws, which explain how the pressure, temperature, volume, and the number of particles in a container of gas are related.

Boyle's law says that if the volume of a gas decreases then the pressure increases. If you squeeze a balloon, reducing its volume, you can feel the pressure of the gas inside it resisting your squeeze.

Charles's law says that a gas expands at a constant rate as its temperature rises. For example, doubling the temperature doubles the gas's volume as long as the pressure does not change.

Avogadro's law says that equal volumes of different gases at the same temperature and pressure will all contain the same number of particles.

The bubbles from this diver's breathing apparatus get bigger because the water pressure around them lessens as they rise towards the surface.

Using solids

Aircraft, like many other things around us, are made from materials called solids.

Nearly all of the materials we see and use every day are solids, including the homes we live in, the furniture inside our homes, all forms of transport from skates to supersonic aircraft, the food we eat, the books we read, the clothes we wear and much, much more.

We can make things with solids that are strong and will keep their shape. Although solids can become liquid if enough heat energy is applied, we tend to use solids that stay solid under normal conditions. Imagine if your clothes suddenly became liquid!

Solid to liquid and back again

Turning solids into liquids makes them easier to shape into the forms we want. Molten metal can be poured into moulds, for example. Once it cools and becomes solid again it can be put to use. Cement is mixed with water, sand and stones to form concrete, which can be poured to form building foundations and dries to give a tough and strong material.

Solid fuels

The most commonly used solid fuel is coal. It is used mainly to produce electricity. It is burned to create heat that is used to turn water into steam, which is then used to spin **turbines**, which generate electricity. Coal is also used to heat buildings and to provide energy for industrial machinery.

Wood has been used as a fuel longer than any other material. Today, it is still an important fuel in some countries where it is used for cooking and heating.

Blacksmiths use coke to produce the heat needed to soften iron so that it can be hammered into shape on the anvil.

Using liquids

Hydroelectric power stations use the energy of moving water to produce electricity.

The study of the way liquids behave is called hydraulics. **Civil engineers** use hydraulics to study the flow of water so they can design water supply systems and sewage systems for cities and towns. Mechanical engineers use hydraulics to design machines such as hydraulic **turbines**, power steering for cars and construction equipment.

Water power

Turbines are large wheels that use the energy of flowing water or steam to power an **electricity generator**.

Hydraulic presses are used for lifting heavy loads and stamping out metal parts. A simple hydraulic press has a **fluid**-filled cylinder containing two **pistons**, one smaller than the other. A force applied to the smaller piston is transferred through the fluid to the larger piston. The brakes in a car work like hydraulic presses. Pressure on the brake pedal is transmitted through a liquid to brake shoes, which press against the car's wheels.

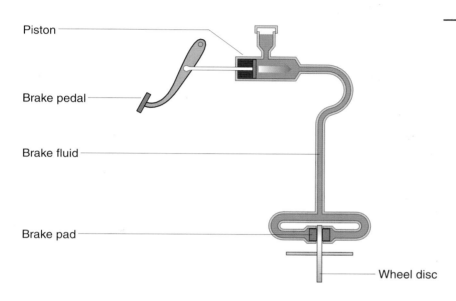

Piston

Brake pedal

Brake fluid

Brake pad

Wheel disc

Pressing on the brake pedal transmits a force through the brake fluid to the brake pads, which press against the wheel.

Lubrication

Liquids such as oil or grease are used as **lubricants**. A thin layer coats the moving parts of a machine, preventing them from rubbing together and therefore reducing friction.

Liquid fuels

Liquid fuels are easy to store and transport. Petrol, diesel oil and kerosene are important liquid fuels. Petrol is used to provide energy for most motor vehicles. Diesel oil powers most trains, ships, and large trucks and kerosene provides the energy for jet aircraft.

Using gases

Some gases are lighter than the mixture of gases that make up the air we breathe. They will rise above it. We can use this natural lifting power to get off the ground by using balloons. Hydrogen is the lightest of all gases and has the greatest lifting power but it is not very safe because it burns easily. Helium is slightly heavier than hydrogen, but it does not burn and so it is much safer. Gas balloons can be used for fun and for science. They have been used to carry scientific instruments for measuring the weather 48 kilometres above ground.

Hot air balloons make good use of the fact that increasing the temperature of a gas makes it less dense.

Gas refrigerator

The first practical refrigerator was built by Frenchman Ferdinand Carré in 1857. Ammonia gas dissolved in water is heated so that the ammonia boils out of the water. The pressure this creates forces the ammonia into a **condenser** where it cools and forms a liquid. It is then **vaporised** again and becomes very cold. Then it passes through the food compartment, cooling the food as it does so. The ammonia is then dissolved in water again and flows back to the start of the cycle. Carré's refrigerator was too big to be used in homes. Modern refrigerators have electric motors and use gases called HCFCs.

Gas fuels

Gas fuels flow easily through pipes and are a good way of providing energy for both homes and businesses. Natural gas is used to heat buildings, cook food and provide energy for industry.

Gas **turbines** use the hot gases from burning fuels such as oil and natural gas to spin the blades of the turbine. Gas turbines are used to power electricity generators, ships and high-speed cars. They are also an important part of the engines in jet aircraft.

Gases become liquids under pressure, which allows them to be stored in convenient containers.

Melting and freezing

The melting point of a substance is the temperature at which it changes from a solid to a liquid. A pure substance will melt at a definite temperature or within a narrow range of temperatures. A mixture might melt across a range of temperatures.

As heat is added to a solid, such as ice, the temperature of the solid increases until it reaches its melting point. At this point the temperature will stop rising, even though more heat is applied. The additional heat gives more energy to the **molecules** in the solid until the **bonds** that hold them together break and the solid melts. The temperature will stay at the melting point until the solid has completely melted.

The pressure of an ice-skater's blade on the ice melts the ice, creating a thin film of water on the surface that allows the skater to glide along.

Melting mixtures

Mixtures do not melt at a specific temperature. The melting point of most simple mixtures differs from that of any of the pure substances in the mixtures. Brass, an **alloy** of copper and zinc, melts over a range of 900°C to 1000°C, although, the melting point of copper is higher than this at 1083.4°C, and that of zinc is much lower at 419.58°C.

Melting points of some common materials

Water	0°C
Iron	1535°C
Mercury	⁻39°C
Oxygen	⁻218°C

Freezing

The freezing point of a substance is the temperature at which it changes from a liquid to a solid, as when water becomes ice. The temperature of the substance remains at this point until all the liquid has been frozen. The freezing point of a substance is the same temperature as its melting point, when it changes from a solid to a liquid.

Gritting the roads in winter works because the freezing point of a liquid is lowered if something is dissolved in it.

Boiling and evaporation

The boiling point of a liquid is the temperature at which it changes into a gas. As the liquid is heated the **particles** it consists of gain more and more energy until eventually they fly off in all directions as a gas.

Why melting and boiling points differ

Substances have different melting and boiling points because the strength of the bonds between their molecules varies. The stronger the bonds the higher the boiling point. For example, water molecules are strongly attracted to one another and it boils at 100°C. Oxygen molecules are not as strongly held together as water molecules and it has a much lower boiling point of -183°C. Some substances have especially strong bonds and boil only at extremely high temperatures. Gold, for example, has a boiling point of 2807°C.

Evaporation

Puddles of water left on the ground after it rains eventually disappear into the atmosphere as water vapour. This is evaporation, the process by which a liquid turns to a vapour without reaching its boiling point.

The boiling point of water at sea level is 100°C, but at 3050 metres above sea level the boiling point is about 90°C. This makes it difficult for mountaineers to make a good cup of tea!

The molecules in a liquid are always moving around and some have enough energy to escape from the forces holding the molecules together at the liquid's surface. The rate of evaporation increases if the liquid is warmed up because more molecules will have enough energy to escape. The evaporating molecules remove energy from the liquid and so its temperature falls. This cooling effect is used by the body as part of its temperature control system, you cool down as sweat **evaporates** from your skin.

Boiling points of some common materials

Material	Boiling point
Water	*100°C*
Iron	*2750°C*
Mercury	*357°C*
Oxygen	*−183°C*

These elephants are using the cooling effect of evaporation to stay cool.

Water

Water is a simple chemical **compound** with remarkable properties. Its chemical formula, H_2O, tells us that each water **molecule** is made up of two **atoms** of hydrogen and one of oxygen. It can exist as a solid (ice), liquid (water), or a gas (water vapour) at everyday temperatures. Pure water is a colourless, odourless, tasteless liquid that freezes at 0°C, and boils at 100°C. Natural water in the environment is never pure. It always contains a variety of dissolved substances.

Water, water everywhere...

The movement of water around the Earth is called the water cycle. Water vapour in the atmosphere **condenses** to fall as rain, flows through rivers and streams into lakes and oceans and is returned to the atmosphere by evaporation.

Water as a solid (ice), liquid (water), and a gas (water vapour on the seal's breath), all at the same time!

Water and life

Water is very important to living organisms. It helps cells to keep their shape and dissolves salts, sugars and other substances that need to be transported around the organism. It also helps to maintain body temperature through perspiration and evaporation.

Properties of water

Water has unusual properties for a molecule of its size. Because of the way its molecules are bonded together it is a very good **solvent** for other substances, such as salts, that are formed from **charged particles**.

Water's unusual properties are due to the hydrogen bonds that link its molecules together.

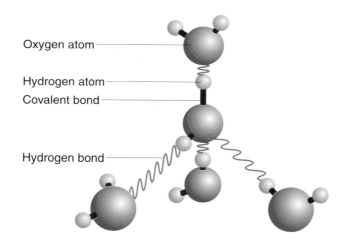

Oxygen atom

Hydrogen atom

Covalent bond

Hydrogen bond

When it is frozen water expands by an eleventh. It also becomes less dense because the atoms of hydrogen and oxygen are linked in such a way that when the water becomes a solid the molecules join up to form a crystal-like pattern that is less dense than water as a liquid. This is why ice floats on water.

Atoms in motion

Particles of matter are never still. The chair you are sitting on might appear solid and unmoving, but the **molecules** from which it is made are constantly vibrating. The physical properties of matter can be explained in terms of the movement of the **atoms** and molecules that make it up. This is called kinetic theory.

Temperature and movement

Temperature is a measure of the energy of movement of the particles in an object. Increased temperature means increased movement.

Chemical kinetics

Chemical kinetics is the study of the rates of chemical reactions. For a reaction to take place the molecules of the elements or compounds involved in the reaction must collide with enough energy to break the **bonds** that join the molecules together and form new ones.

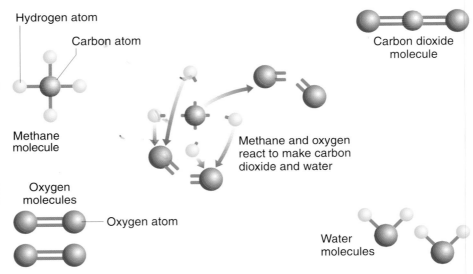

Hydrogen atom

Carbon atom

Carbon dioxide molecule

Methane molecule

Methane and oxygen react to make carbon dioxide and water

Oxygen molecules

Oxygen atom

Water molecules

In order for a chemical reaction to take place the molecules have to collide with each other with sufficient energy to break the bonds that hold them together.

Kinetics and gases

All the explanations we have about the behaviour of gases come from kinetic theory, the idea of molecules in motion. A gas is made up of rapidly moving atoms or molecules. According to kinetic theory, it is the impact of these moving particles on a container holding the gas that accounts for the pressure of the gas.

When the temperature is raised, the molecules gain energy and their speed increases. Because they are now hitting the walls of the container faster and more frequently the pressure increases too. If more gas particles are added or if the volume of the container is reduced, the number of particles hitting the walls at any time increases and so the pressure also increases.

Molecules in a gas are constantly moving in a random way.

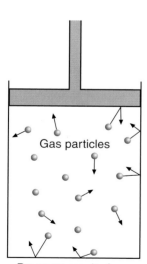

Pressure results from particles striking the sides of a container

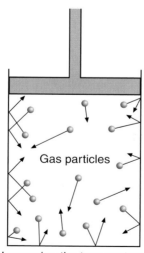

Increasing the temperature increases the pressure as the particles strike more frequently

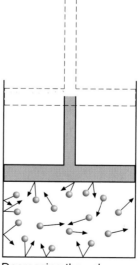

Decreasing the volume increases the pressure as the particles now have a smaller area to strike

The fourth state

In science classes, only three states of matter are commonly described. We have met them all so far.

- solids, which have definite size and shape;
- liquids, which have a definite volume but no definite shape;
- gases, which have no definite size or shape.

If the temperature of a gas is raised to over 10,000°C, the **molecules** of the gas begin to collide with each other so violently that the **bonds** that hold them together are broken apart and they split into individual **atoms**. Some of the atoms can even have **electrons** knocked completely off.

A plasma is a soup of atoms, electrons and ions.

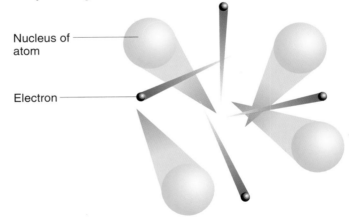

Nucleus of atom

Electron

This produces a gas mixture, consisting of positively **charged** atoms, called **ions**, negatively charged electrons, and atoms with no electric charge. This mixture is called a plasma.

Electric plasma

A plasma is a good **conductor** of electricity. A plasma differs from a gas because it is affected by electricity and magnetism. But because the number of electrons and ions in the plasma are equal they cancel each other out. So, although it has magnetic and electrical properties, a plasma is neutral.

Looking for plasmas

Plasmas exist in the hot hearts of stars. The Sun is a 1.5-million-kilometre ball of plasma, heated by **nuclear reactions** at its core. Above the Earth's atmosphere is the magnetosphere, the magnetic field that surrounds the Earth. Plasma in the magnetosphere shields Earth from cosmic **radiation**. Plasmas can also be found closer to home. Lightning produces a plasma in the atmosphere. When an electric current is passed through neon gas it produces light and plasma.

In a plasma atoms are stripped of electrons, forming a 'soup' of charged particles.

Plasma energy
Scientists are studying ways of creating very hot plasmas in an attempt to harness the energy of stars here on Earth.

Glossary

alloy mixture of two or more metals, or a metal and a non-metal

atom tiny particle from which all materials are made; the smallest part of an element that can exist

bonds forces that hold atoms together in molecules

brittle describes a substance that is hard but which will break or shatter easily

charged having an electric charge

civil engineer an engineer who designs roads, bridges and similar structures

compound a substance that is made up of atoms of two or more elements

condense when a gas becomes a liquid

condenser a piece of apparatus for condensing a gas

conductor something that conducts heat or electricity

crystals solids in which the atoms are arranged in a regular pattern

dense describes a substance in which the atoms or molecules are packed closely together

electricity generators machines for generating electricity

electrons negatively-charged particles that are found in all atoms and that are the main carriers of electrical energy

element a substance that cannot be broken down into simpler substances by chemical reactions, an element is made up of just one type of atom

evaporate change into a vapour or a gas

fluid a substance that has no fixed shape; a gas or a liquid

friction force that acts to slow down or stop objects that are moving against each other

gravity force of attraction between objects

ionized describes an atom or molecule that has gained or lost electrons and so has an overall electric charge

ions an atom or group of atoms that has an electric charge

kinetic energy energy of movement

latent heat heat taken in or given out when a substance changes from one state to another

lubricants substances that are used to reduce friction between moving parts of a machine

mass the amount of matter that something contains

molecules two or more atoms combined together; if the atoms are the same it is an element, if they are different it is a compound

nuclear reactions reactions that involve changes to atoms

particles tiny portions of matter

piston a disc or cylinder that moves up and down inside a tube

pressure a force pushing on a given area

radiation high energy rays or particles; cosmic radiation comes from space

solvent a substance that can dissolve something

sublimation changing from a solid to a gas

turbine a motor with a set of blades that rotate when pushed by a moving stream of liquid or gas

vaporise convert into a vapour or gas

vapour pressure the pressure produced by a liquid as it evaporates

volume the amount of space occupied by something

Index